JOE'S BROS AND THE BUS THAT GOES

Paul Kerensa

Illustrated by Liz and Kate Pope

spck

Now come and meet **Joe**,

and his **squillion** brothers:

Like **Asher** and **Dan**

and **Judah** and . . . others.

With SO many bro's,
A BIG car was a must.
So they took all their trips
in their dad's minibus.

Dad just couldn't help it:

Joe was his favourite.

'Choose a coat, Joe!

And, you know what, I'll pay for it.'

Joe's brothers' coats
were all dark grey, or duller,
So Joe picked a jacket
of every bright colour.

Green sleeves, silver lining,
blue collar, gold top,
Black belt, chocolate buttons:
the best in the shop!

Joe's brothers frowned

at the reds, blues and greens,

Not helped, as they left,

when Joe told them his dreams.

'Hey brothers – I dreamed
that we had sheaves of wheat,
And yours bowed to mine –
like you knelt at my feet!
And the sun, moon and stars,
they bowed too –
who'd have thunk?!'

As he talked, the door closed,

with a *'pffft, beeeeep, clunk!'*

Joe's jacket snagged
on the minibus door –
As the bus *trundled off*,
his coloured coat t o r e .

'Hey guys, wait up!
You're my bros, that's what matters . . .'
But they'd gone. Joe looked down:
dreams and jacket in tatters.

The brothers had sold poor young
Joe down the street –
A long way from home,
he was sad and downbeat.

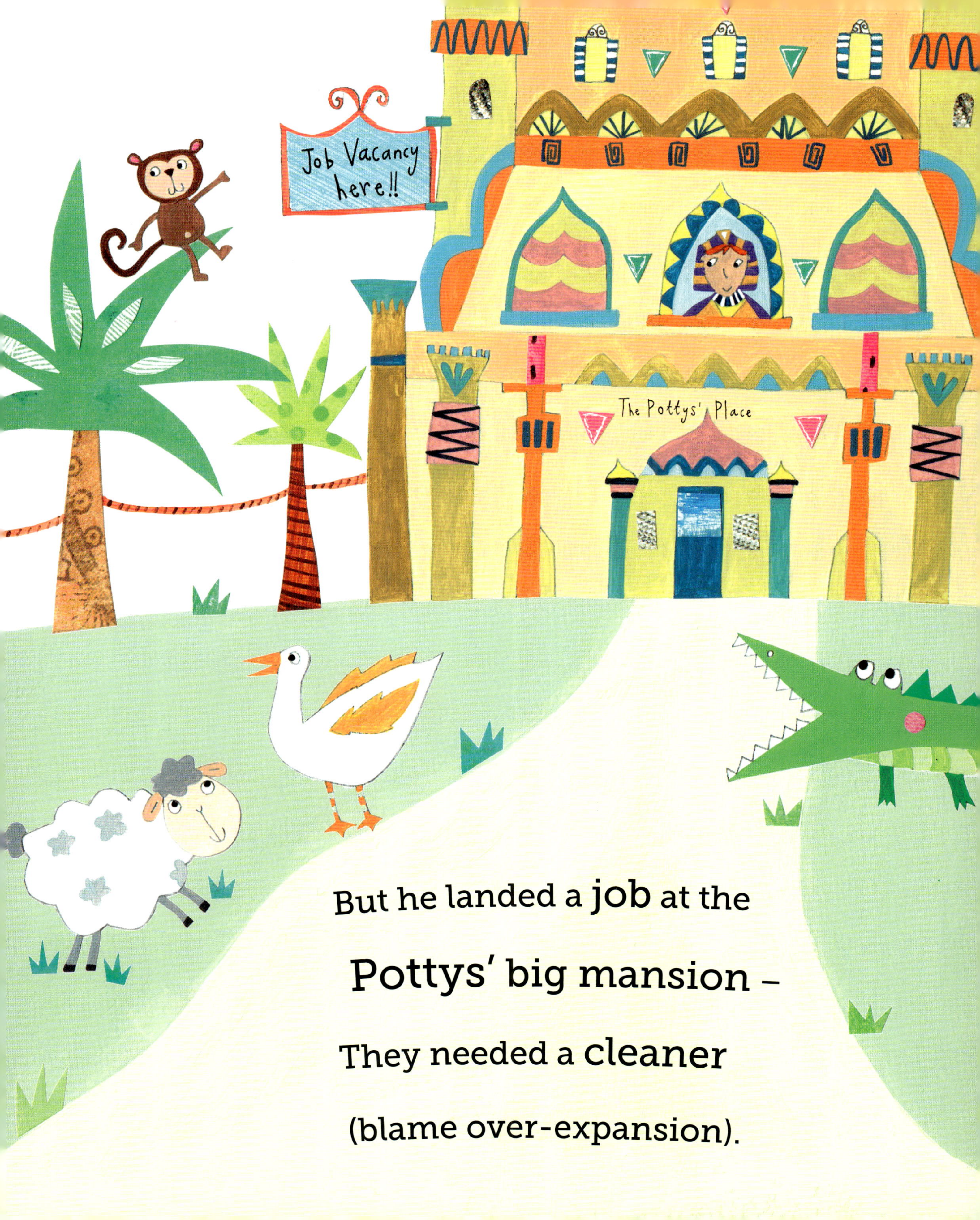

But he landed a job at the

Pottys' big mansion –

They needed a cleaner

(blame over-expansion).

Joe liked Mrs Potty,

liked cleaning her jewellery,

But one day she grabbed him,

for a bit of tomfoolery.

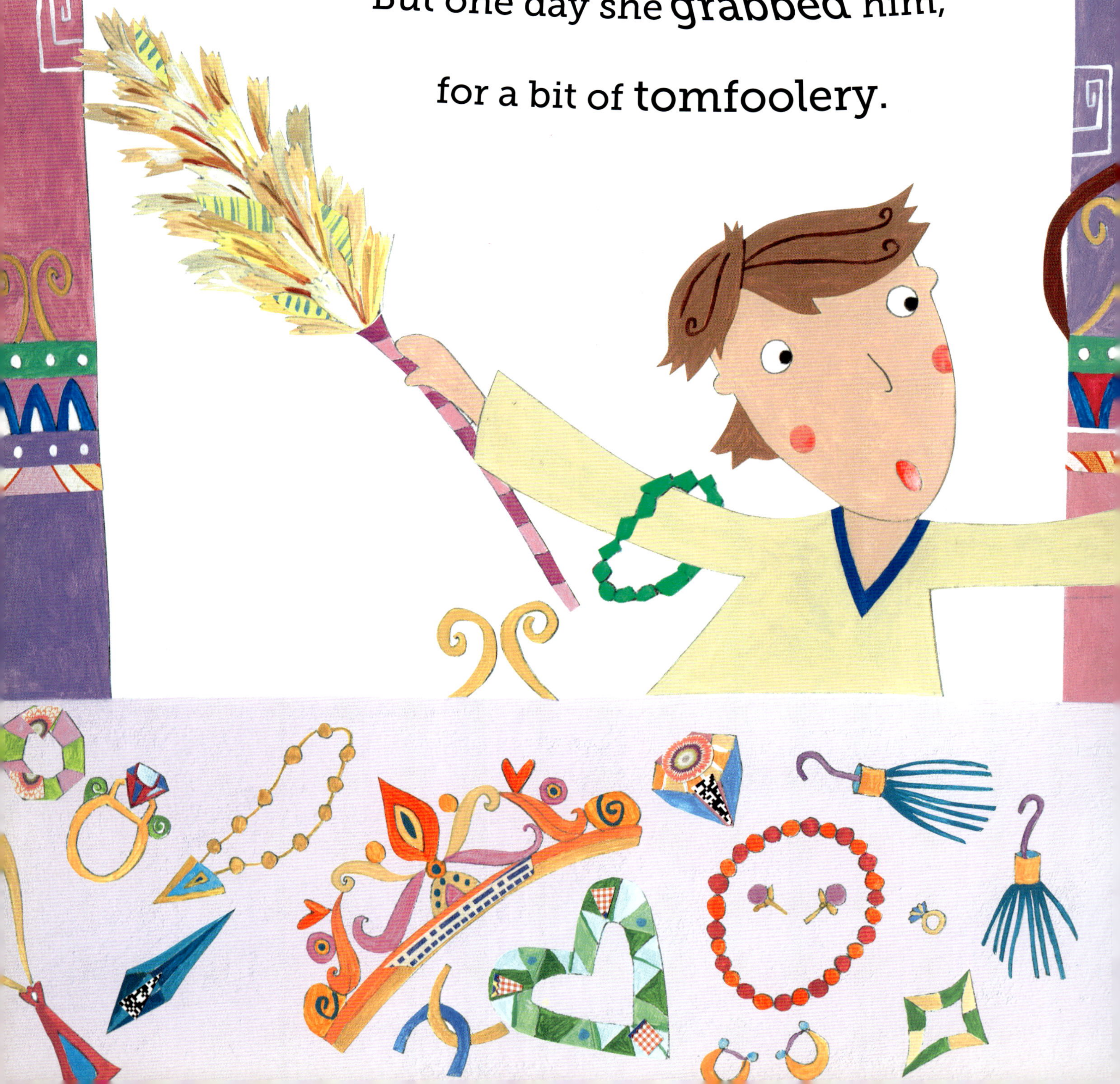

'Come on now, Joe!

I'm just after some kisses!'

So Joe ran off quickly,

pursued by this Mrs.

Out in the street,

a **policeman** was strolling . . .

He spotted the **jewels** that

poor Joe was still holding.

Out stepped Mrs Potty –

she shouted **'Stop, thief!'**

'She *chased* me!' said Joe,

in complete **disbelief**.

The police didn't **trust** him,

so Joe was then **driven**

In a rusty police van,

and taken to **prison.**

His cellmate had worked
for the king as a waiter.
'Hey Joe! I've had dreams.
Could you be my translator?'

'I *dreamed* of these grapes,

and some vines and a tree.'

Joe replied, 'Oh, that means

God says you'll be free!'

'You'll be back in your **job**,

by the king, serving **ale** . . .'

And the next day he was –

but **forgot** Joe in jail.

Years later, a crazy **dream**

bothered the **king**.

Fat cows and **thin** cows –

what did it all mean?

The waiter said,
'I know a man who can tell us!'
The king's finest carriage
brought Joe to the palace.

'Your **dream**,' said Joe,

'means **seven years** of **good harvests**,

But stockpile or next seven years

we'll all **starve**.'

'It's important to store
in a warehouse that's **large.'**
'I will!' said the king,
'Oh and you'll be in **charge.'**

So Joe became **boss** of collecting the **grain**,
For **seven good years** of nice crop-growing **rain**.

The next seven years, the tractors went **quiet** . . .
But thanks to Joe's storage, all ate a **good diet.**

A familiar **bus** came –
Joe's **brothers** were **hungry**,
They'd not **stored** like Joe had,
so travelled cross-country.

But who was this **helpful man**
giving them dinner? **Their brother?**
Last seen in the bus' rear-view mirror?

They *bowed*, but Joe **hugged** them:
'It's me! I'm your brother!
Just now with an apron
of every bright **colour**!'

The brothers
and sun,
moon
and stars
looked and smiled.
But, above all,
God loved what
He'd dreamed
for this child.

First published in Great Britain in 2019

Society for Promoting Christian Knowledge
36 Causton Street, London SW1P 4ST
www.spck.org.uk

British Library Cataloguing-in-Publication Data
A catalogue record for this book is available from the British Library

ISBN 978-0-281-08264-3

1 3 5 7 9 10 8 6 4 2

Typeset and designed by Anna Lubecka, Banana Bear Books

Printed by Imago

Produced on paper from sustainable forests